Zen

How To Live Your Life The Zen Way – Beginners Guide For Zen Meditation

Elias Axmar

Contents

Elias Axmar

Introduction

I want to thank you and commend you for opening the book, Zen: How to Live Your Life the Zen Way – Beginners guide for Zen Meditation".

This book contains actionable information on how to live the Zen way.

Peace and happiness is what all of us desire from deep within, and the good news is that you can make your life completely blissful and peaceful. The perfect way to do that is by following Zen, which is a popular branch of Buddhism.

By following Zen and Zen meditation, you can easily infuse everything happy and positive into your life because Zen helps you cleanse your mind and body of negativities and all the elements that produce negativity. If this intrigues you and you're interested in finding out more about Zen, this guide will serve as your ultimate aide.

This book looks closely into what Zen is, how you can practice it, its benefits along with the challenges you are likely to face while practicing Zen in the start and some wonderful strategies to help you overcome those difficulties. So, get started with it and discover the amazing power of Zen.

Thanks again for opening this book, I hope you enjoy it!

Chapter 1: Understanding Zen And Zen Meditation

Zen is a division of Buddhism, which is a code of life started by Siddharta Gautama Buddha around 2500 years back. The word Zen originated from the Chinese word "Dhyana", which is usually pronounced as "Cha'an". The word means meditation. Translated to Japanese, Ch'an means Zen so Zen simply means seated meditation. The word also means Seon in Korea, Thien in Vietnam and Zen in Japanese.

It is based on the principles and teachings taught by Buddha and emphasizes mainly on meditating regularly and discovering the basic purpose and truth of life. Bodhidharma defined Zen using the following terms:

"A special transmission outside the scriptures;
No dependence on words and letters;
Direct pointing to the mind of man;
Seeing into one's nature and attaining Buddhahood."

So what exactly is Zen Buddhism? Well, Zen Buddhism is a blend of Mahayana Buddhism and Taoism Buddhism, a practice, which was handed down from master to disciple across different generations. The truth is that Zen Buddhism is not a theory, belief, fragment of knowledge or ideology so trying to define it is truly fruitless.

However, you can still describe it as a practical experience that entails using Zazen (refers to sitting meditation- it comes from two terms Za, which means sit and Zen, which means meditation). This means that by adopting the Zen way of life, you will have to resort to meditating regularly to find what life truly means and end all your worries, discomforts and tensions.

Teachings of Zen

The essence of Zen lies in living in today, the present moment and letting go of all your concerns pertinent to your future and regrets, worries and bad memories of the past. It helps you experience the present and every moment it brings with itself. According to Buddha, the basic reason why people are unhappy is because they are forgetful of what they are blessed with and are lost in the materialistic world because of their uncontrollable and incessant desires.

When we become lost in this world, we are either worried about what might happen to us, or what we might lose in the future if we don't act in a certain way right now; or we are disturbed by our past- something that has already happened and cannot be changed. We continue ruminating on these thoughts and begin locking them inside our minds. This leads to having a negative and unhealthy mindset, which makes us do all that which isn't healthy and beneficial for us. We backbite, indulge in gossiping, think negatively of others, adopt unhealthy and illegitimate means of earning, become involved in bad habits and do everything that has a bad influence on us. Though we feel we are happy the way we are living, but in reality, we are completely dissatisfied with our lives. We stay depressed quite often and become so involved in negative actions, behaviors, and thinking that we find it difficult to let go. This increases our stress, anxiousness and tension and makes us go through different sorts of sufferings.

Our suffering is exactly what makes life miserable and this is precisely where Zen comes in handy. It teaches us to slowly disengage ourselves from everything that makes us unaware of our beautiful present and avoid it, so we can acknowledge our blessings and be thankful for them. The best way to be mindful of the present and acknowledge it is by improving your concentration and focus, which can be attained by the amazing practice of meditation. This is precisely why Zen revolves around meditation.

Digging Deeper Into Zen

To better understand the purpose of practicing Zen, it is important that you get some knowledge of the fundamentals Zen is based on. Zazen has its roots in Buddhism, which has its basis in the 'Four Noble Truths' and the 'Eightfold Path.' Let us find out what these are.

The Four Noble Truths

As you already know, Buddha developed Buddhism. Buddha's original name was Sidharta Gautama and he was born in a noble family as a prince. Although he lived a life enriched with luxuries, he was never satisfied by it. He always found people going through some sort of suffering which greatly upset him and he decided to abandon his lavish life and go in search of the true meaning of life. His search was quite a long one, but eventually enabled him understand that life revolves around four noble truths.

Truth of Dukha

The first truth aka the truth of dukkha states that each one of us faces some kind of suffering in our lives. Suffering is broadly characterized into mental suffering and physical suffering. Mental or emotional grief refers to the emotional pain we go through upon losing anything important to us, or going through a traumatic episode. Physical suffering points to all the physical pain and misery we go through. From the time we are born until we die, we go through various kinds of physical pain.

The objective of this truth is to help you realize that suffering exists in the world and it cannot be completely evaded. If you want to attain serenity in life, you first need to acknowledge the presence of suffering and then work towards saving yourself from it. Yes, it will touch you at some point, but you can protect yourself from its impact with the help of Zen.

Truth of Reason Behind Dukha

The second truth aka the truth pointing out the reasons behind dukkha or suffering explains why we suffer. We suffer because we are ignorant about the purpose of our lives and because we are constantly craving for materialistic pleasures. We crave for money, food, clothes, shelter, popularity, entertainment, better health, abundance, wealth, holidays, luxuries and everything that we feel is going to make our lives better. The desire for more makes us run after the worldly objects and since we cannot acquire everything all the time, we end up becoming unhappy. Even if we did manage to get everything we desire, there would come a time when it would start to bore us and we would again become upset. Hence, craving ends in some sort of suffering.

Being ignorant means not having the ability to identify the real truth of everything. We don't know what our purpose in this world is which makes us develop the wrong core values and attach ourselves to the wrong things, which makes us suffer. Therefore, to end our sufferings, we need to end the cause that leads towards suffering.

Truth of the Culmination of All Sufferings

The third truth aka the truth related to the culmination of sufferings explains that all our sufferings can be terminated if we become determined to end our desires and cravings. By ending our grief and misery, we can reach the amazing state of nirvana, which is a state characterized by contentment, enlightenment and peace. Buddha was able to achieve it via deep meditation.

Truth of the Middle Path

The fourth truth aka the truth of the path that helps end sufferings provides you with the kind of life you need to adopt to eradicate all your problems. This path is referred to as the eightfold noble path or the middle way because it gives you eight factors that you need to follow to live a balanced and harmonious life.

Eightfold Noble Path

Also referred to as the middle way, eightfold path and the middle path, the eightfold noble path sets out eight guidelines that you need to fulfill to cleanse your mind and body of desires, wrongdoings, ill thinking and suffering. The eight factors are often divided into three categories: wisdom (which consists of the first two factors), ethical conduct (comprising of the third, fourth and fifth points) and concentration (which contains the last three factors.) These eight factors are:

1. Right View: The first factor is right view, also known as 'samma ditthi' in Sanskrit. It means to correct your view about everything and discover the truth related to things. Quite often, we accept things the way they are provided to us without finding out whether or not what we are told is correct. This makes us place our faith on the wrong things and gives birth to a cycle of wrongdoings. As your view about something induces your mindset, it is important that you correct it first.

2. Right Intention: It is the second factor, which is referred to as 'samma sankappa' in Sanskrit. Right intention or right thought refers to correcting your thoughts and infusing positivity into your thinking pattern. Your

thoughts need to be full of compassion and love for the humankind and reject everything that contains negativity.

3. Right Speech: The third factor is right speech, which is known as samma vacca in Sanskrit. To acquire the right speech, you need to shun gossiping, slanderous talk, backbiting and every sort of negativity from your speech.

4. Right Action: The fourth factor 'right action' is also known as 'samma kammanta' in Sanskrit and advises us to abandon all sorts of wrong behaviors and negative actions that inflict any sort of harm on us or the ones around us. This includes illegitimate sexual misconduct, illegal actions, murder, destructive actions and from taking any illegitimate object from anyone.

5. Right Livelihood: Right livelihood is referred to as 'samma ajiva' in Sanskrit and refers to adopting the right means of earning. This means you need to abstain from all types of professions that can infuse negativity in your life. This includes prostitution, dealing in intoxicants, dealing in weapons, dealing in flesh and dealing in any kind of poisonous substance.

6. Right Effort: The sixth factor is right effort, known as 'samma vayama' in Sanskrit. It means that your energy and effort towards everything needs to be right and positive. Your effort can only be correct when you start adopting the five aforementioned factors in your life.

7. Right Mindfulness: Right mindfulness is the seventh factor and is known as 'samma satti' in Sanskrit. Right

mindfulness means to live in a state of mindfulness, which as described above means to be aware of the present and live in. Only when you dwell in the present, are you able to relax your mind and clear it of all types of upsetting thoughts.

8. Right Concentration: The last factor is right concentration, referred to as 'samma samadhi' in Sanskrit. It means that you must be completely focused on the subject under consideration and when your concentration is right, you are able to understand things better and become more mindful of your thoughts.

If you follow these eight factors and incorporate them into your life, you can turn your chaotic life into a blissful and peaceful one. The key to acquiring these factors is by getting insight into your thoughts because Buddha clearly stated that everything we do and whoever we are is because of our thoughts. Therefore, to find out what's wrong with you and to improve yourself, you need to correct your thoughts, which can be easily done with the help of Zazen. Let us now quickly find out how Zen can improve your quality of life.

Chapter 2: How Zen Improves Your Quality Of Life?

Zen gives you an opportunity to find out who you are by helping you understand your thoughts.

'We are what we think. All that we are arises with our thoughts. With our thoughts, we make the world.'- Buddha

This meaningful quote by Buddha beautifully describes why we become upset or happy, sad or jubilant, positive or negative and stressed or peaceful. It is your thoughts that shape your emotions and feelings, and when you feel a certain way, you behave in a specific manner as well. Therefore, the root of everything that is right or wrong is your thoughts, and to correct everything that is wrong in your life, you need to fix your thinking pattern, which can be attained by practicing Zen. So, how can you do this?

Identify the Negative Thoughts

You are unable to identify the various negative thoughts going on inside your mind because mostly, the brainwaves in your brain correspond to the gamma (highest frequency), beta (high frequency) and alpha (moderate frequency) ranges. When your brainwaves are in the gamma and beta ranges, you are actively involved in thinking, decision making, learning and it is these brainwaves that are extremely prevalent in people suffering from anxiety, depression, stress and other emotional and mental disorders. When your brainwaves correspond to the alpha frequency, you are relaxed, but not completely aware of your thoughts.

However, when you perform Zen, you are able to slow down the frequency of your brainwaves and are able to give your thoughts some rest. You are able to make them enter into the theta (low frequency) and delta (lowest frequency) ranges, which calms down your active thinking and helps you observe and analyze your thoughts. The moment, the pace of the thoughts entering and leaving your mind slows down, you're able to spot the ones inducing negativity, which is the first step towards correcting yourself.

Replace Unhealthy Thoughts with Healthy Ones

By constantly practicing Zazen, you are able to have control over yourself because you are able to manage your thoughts. This helps you eliminate every ounce of negativity from your mind and develop a healthy, happy and positive mindset.

Gain Peace of Mind

With time, you are able to reinforce your positive thinking. As the positivity inside you strengthens, you are able to eliminate all sorts of wrongdoings from your life and improve it. When negativities are discarded, your sufferings end and the end of sufferings is nirvana. By meditating regularly and with full concentration, you are able to attain nirvana- complete peace of mind.

'To enjoy good health, to bring true happiness to one's family, to bring peace to all, one must first discipline and control one's own mind. If a man can control his mind he can find the way to Enlightenment, and all wisdom and virtue will naturally come to

him.'- Buddha

Spread Love Around You

When you become peaceful and learn the purpose of your life, you realize that to live a complete and pleasant life, you must help others and educate them about improving their life just the way you did. This motivates you to spread kindness and love around, and radiate happiness.

'Thousands of candles can be lighted from a single candle, and the life of the candle will not be shortened. Happiness never decreases by being shared.'- Buddha

Improve Your Personal and Professional Lives

Zazen also helps you improve your relationships, personal life and professional life as well. It helps you focus on what you have now and make the best use of it, which helps you do the right thing at the right time. When your focus improves, you become more alert and manage time better, which helps you procrastinate less and improves your productivity.

In addition, meditation helps you live in present and value what you have now. This makes you cognizant of the importance of your loved ones, making you value them more and fix all that you have destroyed. Hence, with the help of Zen, you can easily bring back love, trust, sincerity and happiness in your relationship.

Chapter 3: Zen In Daily Life

The two main forms of practicing Zen are doing Zazen, which is seated meditation and correcting your daily life. We will begin with Zen in daily life, so you can learn how to improve your daily routine at home and workplace, to live a better life.

Live Each Moment Completely

Zen practitioners believe in living in the present, which is, only possible if you live every moment completely and as if there's no tomorrow. To live every moment, you need to savor it and experience it fully. Here's how you can learn to live every moment to its fullest.

Do Everything Completely

Whatever you do, make sure to do it completely and put your mind fully to it. For instance, if you are making a project report, or doing laundry, then your mind should focus on precisely what you are doing and think of no other chore. If the thought of any other task pops up in your mind, just jerk your head and realign your attention on what you are doing. Make sure to finish the current task completely and then head over to the next task. This helps you slow down your pace and not do everything in a hurry. When you do things in a relaxed manner, you are able to enjoy them and live in the moment.

Do Things Slowly

Whatever you are doing, ensure to do it very slowly. Be deliberate in your actions and know what you are doing, which is only possible when you perform task gradually and slowly. Quite often, when we do something, we don't even realize that we are carrying out that action because our mind is lost somewhere else. This happens because we aren't dwelling in the moment. To return your thoughts to the present, you need to calm down your mind and this is exactly why you need to do your tasks deliberately and slowly.

Accept Your Mind and Body as One

Zen monks do not believe in dualism, which states that your mind and body are two separate entities. They believe that your mind and body are one and need to work as a unit. So when you practice Zen, you need to learn to transcend dualism. Letting go of dualism helps align your mind and body together. So, your body acts in the way your mind thinks. This means if you are thinking positively, you will be behaving positively. Hence, to correct your actions and thinking, transcending dualism is very important. This is how you can achieve this goal.

Do Less and One Task at a Time

Whether you are at home or at the office, you need to schedule your day in a manner that you don't overburden yourself. Zen monks do a lot of work, but they never fill their schedule with myriads of tasks at once. The reason why their minds and bodies are aligned is because their focus and concentration is incredibly strong. To improve your focus, you need to do one task at a time. When you do less and one thing at one time, you concentrate better on it which helps your mind and body behave in a similar manner.

Inject Mindfulness into Everything You Do

Whatever you do, make sure to be mindful of it. By becoming aware of what you're doing, you make your mind and body work in a similar manner which aligns them and helps you transcend dualism. This means that you need to be mindful of eating, drinking, doing any chore, driving, playing with your kids and basically everything that you do. Here's how you can do that.

- Mindful Eating: When you take a bite, chew it very slowly and take in the flavor of each piece of food that you are chewing and swallowing. This makes you focus completely on what you are eating, be mindful of that act and be appreciative of the yummy food you're eating.

- Mindful Driving: While driving your car, or riding any transport, savor each moment of the ride. Switch off the music and focus completely on the road and the views you come across. Absorb every view as if you're seeing it for the first time and enjoy it.

- Mindful Writing: While working on any written task in your workplace, put your mind into it. Observe the way you are moving the pen, sense what muscles become activated when you write and focus on each word that you are penning down. This helps you immerse yourself fully into the task and do it properly, completely and mindfully. Practice this strategy with everything you do, including cleaning, cooking, thinking, observing, walking, running and relaxing.

- 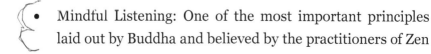 Mindful Listening: One of the most important principles laid out by Buddha and believed by the practitioners of Zen

13

is to inquire everything and not accept things the way they are given to you. This means you need to investigate into things and one basic step of doing that is practicing mindful listening. Mostly, we listen to things with a biased mindset and don't listen to them in a rational and unbiased manner. Mindful listening helps you understand and hear things the way they are without forming your own judgment of them. To practice it, select any musical piece you have never heard and listen to it until the end. Make sure not to form any opinion of it based on the artist's name or character, and focus on the music and lyrics of the piece. With constant practice, you will be able to listen and perceive things the way they are and become more alert, which will automatically help your mind and body come into line with one another.

Practice these simple exercises in your routine life, so you can come closer to living life the Zen way and can become peaceful.

Chapter 4: Zazen- How To Perform Zazen

Let's now us focus on the second and extremely important element of Zen: seated meditation. Zazen is the essence of Zen and can help you kill everything unhealthy and unconstructive in your mind and help you develop a sense of peace, contentment, and fulfillment. Let us find out how you can perform Zazen.

Step #1- Get a Zafu

Get a zafu, which is a small, comfy pillow. It is used for helping you raise a little off the ground, so you can sit comfortably. If sitting on the floor isn't a problem for you, then you need not get a zafu.

Step #2- Get into Gear

Next, you need to get into gear, which means choose a comfortable sitting position. The commonly used positions in zazen include:

- Burmese Position: To get into this position, you need to cross your legs, keeping your knees flat on the ground.

Your left ankle needs to be in front of the right one, or the right in front of the left one. Make sure your ankle isn't over the other.

- Half Lotus: Also known as 'hankafuza', the half lotus pose requires you to place your left foot onto your right thigh. You need to gently tuck in your right leg beneath the left thigh.

Half Lotus

- Full Lotus: Full lotus, or 'kekkafuza' is an extremely stable position. You place your foot onto its opposite thigh. It is difficult for beginners, so you can start off with the Burmese or half lotus pose and slowly work your way towards full lotus. If you suffer from knee or joint pain, it is best you don't practice this pose.

- Seiza: Seiza pose is the kneeling position. You kneel on the ground and rest your hips on the ankles.

Seiza
position

- Chair Pose: To practice this pose, sit on a comfortable chair and ensure to keep your spine straight.

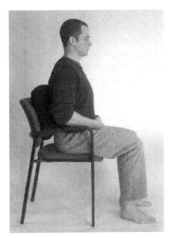

- Standing Pose: Though zazen is basically seated meditation, it doesn't compel you to meditate while sitting only. If you cannot remain seated for long periods, you can stand up. Keep your legs and feet straight and your feet should be shoulder width apart. Keep your hand on your belly, preferably right one over the left one and meditate.

Step #3- Practice Cosmic Mudra

Next, you can practice the cosmic mudra. This is optional, which is why the word 'can' has been used here. Mudra is a hand position and helps you achieve amazing results in your body. It is believed that different nerves in your hand connect with various parts of your brain. By using these connections, you can produce the result you desire, such as better health, good body, great confidence, love, abundance, focus and mindfulness.

The cosmic mudra is excellent for beginners of zazen as it helps your mind relax, improves your awareness of things and increases your mindfulness. To practice it, open your hands and bring your right hand forward. Now open your left palm and place it on the right one and touch both your right and left thumbs with each other.

Step #4- Clear Your Mind and Focus on Your Breath Only

Next, you need to close your eyes. This is optional too, but best for beginners since it helps avoid distractions. Then, clear your mind of all sorts of thoughts and focus only on your breath.

Step #5- Count Your Breath

When your mind becomes clear, start counting every inhalation and exhalation. Count until you reach ten.

Step #6- Begin Again if Your Mind Wanders

If your find your thoughts wandering off, you need to start counting again. For instance, you have reached five, but you find the thought of lunch entering your mind, then restart your counting. Keep doing it until no distracting thought bothers you.

Step #7- Count Inhalation and Exhalation as One

When you become successful in getting to ten frequently without experiencing any intruding and disturbing thoughts, you need to stop counting your inhalation and exhalation separately and count them as one breath. This won't happen on day one and it will take you a while to get there. So, don't worry, just keep going. Once you reach this point, meditate for at least 15 minutes. Till the time you don't reach this point, just practice until step 6 for about ten minutes daily. With practice and patience, you will get to step 7 soon.

Exit Meditation

After you have meditated, you need to slowly open your eyes. Get up and stretch your arms and legs. This helps escalate your heartbeat and blood pressure to the normal rate.

Important Points to Remember

There are a few important things you need to take care of when exercising zazen.

- Make sure to meditate for 10 to 15 minutes daily in the first week. Start increasing your session's duration by 5 minutes after two days in the second week. Keep increasing it until you reach 45 to 60 minutes.

- Breathe Naturally: Remember to breathe in your natural, normal way. You don't need to increase or decrease its pace. Zazen is just about finding stillness and peace, which can be easily done by focusing on your breath.

- Explore the Silence: When you are able to attain a stillness in your thoughts, you need to start exploring. Zazen is about finding peace within yourself and uncovering the hidden awareness of everything. This is exactly what helped Buddha acquire nirvana and can do the same for you too. To explore stillness, you need to take one thought at a time and scrutinize it until you know every detail related to it.

Follow these steps to start practicing zazen. Make sure to be consistent in your practice because consistency can help you move closer to your ultimate goal: enlightenment.

Chapter 5: Challenges Faced While Practicing Zen And Strategies To Overcome Them

Zazen is undoubtedly an amazing practice, but not something that you can easily tune yourself into. As a beginner, you are likely to face a few challenges in the start. Let us look at the difficulties novices go through when performing Zen and how you can overcome these problems.

Becoming Impatient

Zazen requires patience. You need to really calm your mind and relax yourself to find the stillness and then explore it. This requires patience. Since you are accustomed to doing everything hastily, sitting calmly in a pose for even 10 minutes would become annoying for you and you would start losing your patience. As a starter, this is the biggest challenge you're going to face. However, you can easily resolve it.

Firstly, you need to acknowledge your impatience the moment you start experiencing it. If you experience a distracting thought and you find yourself losing your patience while meditating, acknowledge that you are becoming impatient in your mind. This helps you realize you're facing a problem that you need to deal with. Next, you need to bring in your mind the benefits of meditating and weigh them against your impatience. While you exhale, envision your impatience going out of your body. Practice this until you start regaining your patience. With time, you will easily be able to become more tolerant.

Ending the Session Quickly

One thing you must understand is that meditation is not just about finding the peace and stillness. It is about doing that of course, but it is also about enjoying that peace and savoring it. Quite often, beginners tend to cut their practice short the moment they start feeling calm and peaceful. This is the biggest mistake they make. To acquire nirvana, you need to dig deeper into the state of peace and if you stop your practice right when you find peace, you'll never be able to go forward. As a starter, you will be tempted to end your session when you become calm, but you must not do that.

To overcome this challenge, you need to take each moment as it comes. Tell yourself that you are going to meditate for ten more seconds. Keep doing things until you have expanded a 15-minute session to a 17-minute one. This will help prolong your session and increase your patience. As a result, you will be able to explore the calmness.

Feeling Drowsy

Losing focus and feeling drowsy are two big challenges faced by novices when meditating. You cannot meditate and focus easily when you become drowsy and feel sleepy. Hence, make sure to sleep properly for at least seven consecutive hours daily, so you wake up fresh every morning and are enthusiastic about your meditation session.

By following the guidelines, you will soon be able to tackle the challenges successfully and become excellent at Zen. Remember to practice a lot. The more you practice, the better you'll be able to meditate and the happier your life will become.

Conclusion

Zen is indeed a great way to live your life and find the peace missing out in your life. However, living it fully is only possible when you are committed to improving yourself and your life for the better. So make that commitment now, stick to it and keep following this guide to unlock your inner peace.

Thank you again for downloading this book!

I hope this book was able to help you to know how to live a Zen life.

The next step is to embrace Zen in your life, as this is the only way you are going to enjoy the benefits that come with embracing Zen.

If you have enjoyed this book, please be sure to leave a review and a comment to let us know how we are doing so we can continue to bring you quality ebooks.

Thank you and good luck!

Preview of Mindfulness: "The Mindfulness Meditation Guide for a Mindful and Stress-Free Life"

This book is a guide that is intended to help you achieve a mindful and stress-free life through the concepts of mindfulness meditation.

Here, mindfulness meditation will be thoroughly discussed. It addresses the fact that there are a handful of reasons why you should appreciate the benefits of mindfulness. While others want a defense against the overload of trivial matters, some aim to be mindful for a sense of inner peace. Some just wish to relax and take a break from most of their worries. With all the people you talk to, the obligations that need attention, and all the other demands of everyday life, the knowledge on mindfulness can be beneficial.

Regardless of personal reason, avoid setting aside the importance of reaching a state of mindfulness. It clears the blurry sights of the current moments, and it opens your eyes to essential matters – both the mundane and the extravagant. Apart from helping you sort out your priorities, it lets you appreciate the reality of the present. Overall, it can reward you with a stress-free life. But, how exactly do you reach the state? You're about to find out.

Chapter 1 – Understanding Mindfulness

If awareness of the present situation is your pursuit, honing your mental well-being should be the focus. Instead of letting chaos, pessimism, and negativity get the best of you, be motivated in achieving mindfulness through mindfulness meditation. To do that, your end necessitates *commitment*. A transformed state of improved mental concentration is one of those things you can't get overnight. You should know that there are barely any shortcuts along the way – especially if you believe you're severely out of shape mentally.

Avoid letting frustrations win over you. Begin with a *roll up your sleeves approach* in understanding the concept of mindfulness meditation. As heaps of discussions featured in psychological science journals go, remind yourself that it can take a while. Taking the long and perhaps, difficult, path may sometimes exhaust you but making small steps can be incredibly rewarding, especially for the long haul. For all you know, it may even be the best way to go at it for you.

Origin & Development

Mindfulness meditation, as adapted from the known practices of traditional and Vietnamese Buddhists in the 1500s (B.C.E.), is the translation of the term *sati*. It describes the process of gaining a whole *new level of wisdom, awareness*, and *kindness* through relaxation. Like the reputation of Buddhists in the ancient days, an individual can live with peace and happiness. The idea is simply to transform his life; it's up to him to make sure that he is designed for a less crowded existence by gradually eliminating unimportant affairs.

Often, due to its adapted nature, mindfulness meditation is compared to most types of meditation techniques. Practices such as *zazen, vipassana, vedic and yogic,* and *metta* are sometimes thought to be similar to mindfulness meditation. Since all of these techniques require focus and promise a stress-free life, the generic definition is understandable.

However, upon closer look, there's a distinguishing factor between mindfulness meditation and other types of meditation; the former is simpler. As the concept of mindfulness meditation proposes, the importance of recognizing practical and straightforward means shouldn't be set aside. Just like in many Western traditions, the power to react and respond is more instrumental during the anticipation of results. When you are drawn to view the world negatively, all you need to do is take a little while to breathe in the good. The solution is to be aware and to pay more attention to the benefits, as opposed to the setbacks. Granted, matters will turn around eventually and you will have a crisp picture of the present situation.

The Three Aspects of Mindfulness

As you meditate for mindfulness, first things first: did you know that there are three different aspects of mindfulness? There are. And, according to numerous mental health psychologists, the practice lets you appreciate the way of the Tibetan monks; meditation can require *solitude*. This is because the road to a collected nature can be multiple times as challenging without total concentration.

While the abilities to stay still and to show undivided focus are essential, the goal of mindfulness meditation is for permanent results. You can't be successful in the process if you're not open to the other foundations. The approach is rather thorough because the idea is to treat both the physical and the mental sides. It argues that achieving a relaxed state is supposed to be done appropriately; it's supposed to be more than just a momentary attempt.

Moreover, the three aspects of mindfulness meditation serve as a reminder that although face-value says so, achieving mindfulness through meditation is not an effortless task. The assumptions that say differently may only come from a beginner's point of view. Those who are in the middle of the practice? They are not oblivious to struggles of sorts on the road. Since it requires discipline, be sure to have unwavering motivation. Always show enthusiasm in replenishing the level of motivation to reach your ultimate goal.

The three aspects:

1. Attitude

   Attitude is an aspect of mindfulness that reveals the significance of acknowledging different characters. It reminds you that in your progress toward successful mindfulness meditation, you should be familiar with certain positive behaviors such as *kindness, integrity, acceptance,* and *curiosity.* As you aim to be mindful, are you also whole-hearted? While you want to invite the good, you should learn to breathe it out in return - for the sake of others.

2. Attention

The aspect of mindfulness meditation that addresses the importance of attentiveness is referred to as attention. To be at peace with yourself, be ready to make room for both the inner and the outer experiences. Since mindfulness describes awareness, this aspect tells you to have the initiative. Just because an object is around you doesn't mean you have to be around it, too. While you are fully aware of your environment, know which elements are worthy of your attention.

3. Intention

Intention is the aspect of mindfulness meditation that allows you to realize your intentions. The aim to achieve a stress-free state is a vague intent; it is broad and usually, it conceals a main and a bigger purpose. By recognizing such purpose, you become aware of honest desires, as well as apparent and unapparent concerns.

Since its strength empowers the drive to reach your ultimate goal, make intention a priority. Remember that it is an important aspect of mindfulness meditation. You can use your intention to polish your determination. For instance, does your main intention involve getting less irritated by a co-worker? Do you need help studying for exams? Are you struggling to keep afloat with your busy schedule? The knowledge of your true desires can cheer you on.

Benefits of Mindfulness & Mindfulness Meditation

As a Harvard research explains, one of the main benefits of mindfulness is the offer to experience unparalleled happiness. The set-up of the study involves two groups: (1) the group that is composed of individuals with hectic schedules and who spent more than 50 hours at work, and (2) the group that is composed of individuals with laid-back lifestyles and who had way too much time on their hands. It revealed that the 2nd group, the participants who had (more than enough) time to notice their surroundings, was the group of happy folks.

Mindfulness meditation, therefore, is a great means of teaching you to adopt a balanced life, as well as finding out what makes you happy. As the psychologists from the prominent school say, it is by learning to have time, and using that time wisely to focus on the essentials that can lead toward the core nature of personal happiness.

The other benefits of mindfulness meditation:

- You can start distancing yourself from unhelpful and toxic situations. While it is not always the easiest task, it lets you learn to take initiative. It makes you discover sensible reasons to flee scenarios that can cause harm to your mental well-being.

- You can discover factors that can trigger stress. You begin to identify which of the elements in your life, however disguised they may be, are no longer fruitful.

- You won't misunderstand vague situations. Instead of the indecisiveness to enter predicaments, you can easily determine whether or not an environment is appropriate.

- You know the way to achieve peace of mind. Since mindfulness teaches honesty, you become familiar with your true self. You start to get rid of potentially harmful desires.

- You learn selflessness and compassion since you understand the predicament of others. You become a better person who sees the best in others, instead of somebody who dwells on *anger, jealousy,* and *insecurity.*

You know better than to make impulsive decisions. You learn to think about your actions carefully. Since there are possible unwanted consequences, you learn to say no to certain situations.

Search for this book on Amazon to check it out. You can also visit my author page on Amazon – Elias Axmar.

Preview of: Buddhism

How To Practice Buddhism In Your Everyday Life

I want to thank you and commend you for opening the book, *"Buddhism: How to Practice Buddhism in Your Everyday Life"*.

This book contains actionable information on how to practice Buddhism in your daily life.

'Better than a thousand hollow words is one word that brings peace.'- Buddha

This beautiful, meaningful quote by Buddha, the founder of Buddhism sums up the basic essence of Buddhism. This book is going to help you better understand what Buddhism is, how it can benefit you, and how you can apply it in your routine life.

Some people refer to Buddhism as a religion, whereas many others call it a way of life and doing things the way they are. Whether it is a religion or not, it preaches peace and it provides you with guidelines that can help you live your life peacefully, happily and successfully. Buddhism provides you with deep information related to the worldly pleasures, your desires, and everything that prevents you from acquiring inner peace and happiness. Moreover, it also guides you on how you can battle all your obstructions, both the inner and outer ones, to gain complete peace of mind.

If you want to improve your understanding of Buddhism, you have landed at the right place. Continue reading this book to find out how Buddhism can be of help to you.

Thanks again for opening this book.

Chapter 1: Buddhism-Detailed Insight Into Buddhism And How It Came Into Being

Buddhism is a philosophy, some refer to it as a religion, or a faith, that comprises of numerous beliefs, spiritual practices and traditions based primarily on the teachings of Gautama Buddha. Let us dig deeper into this and find out more about Buddhism.

How Did Buddhism Come into Being?

Buddhism was founded by Siddharta Gautama Buddha, who is also known as 'Buddha', which means the awakened one. Sidharta Gautama was born around 2600 years back as a prince in a wealthy family that ruled a small area located near the current border shared by India and Nepal. He enjoyed all the luxuries of life and lived a lavish life. Despite all the comforts, Sidharta always felt a certain uneasiness and seldom found himself peaceful.

Search for the book on Amazon for more.

Made in the USA
San Bernardino, CA
22 February 2018